86

RUSSIAN ICONS

PETITE ENCYCLOPÉDIE
DE L'ART

ACHEVÉ D'IMPRIMER EN JANVIER 1967
PAR LES IMPRIMERIES DE BOBIGNY
POUR LES ILLUSTRATIONS
ET PAR L'IMPRIMERIE J.-M. MONNIER
POUR LE TEXTE

RUSSIAN ICONS

BY

JEAN A. KEIM

TUDOR PUBLISHING CO.

NEW-YORK

3, 29. 76

Russian icons made a belated entry into the history of world art. From their first appearance in the 11th century until the beginning of the 20th century, they were regarded simply as religious pictures. After the 16th century, a large number of them were protected by a metal cover, often decorated with precious stones, which only left visible the face and hands of the person depicted. Most of them were blackened with varnish, which was deteriorating, and smoke from the lamp that burnt perpetually in front of each image. When art historians removed this dark layer, they often discovered icons that had been repainted repeatedly through the centuries in a contemporary style, but under these successive layers of more or less recent date there appeared images of an unfamiliar and rare beauty. The exhibition of Ancient Russian Art at Moscow in 1913, where icons were on show for the first time, was a staggering revelation to its visitors.

The Revolution of October 1917 brought countless works into the museums, which had been lost in churches or had been collected privately by art-lovers with tastes in advance of their time. Russian scholars began the enormous labour of restoration and renovation so that today the principal museums of the U.S.S.R. possess some marvellous treasures, particularly the Tretyakov Gallery at Moscow and the Russian Museum at Leningrad. Unfortunately, works of any value are rare outside Russia and, moreover, the Russian icon is still the preserve of a few specialists, when it should be known by all who appreciate beauty because it belongs to the artistic heritage of humanity.

By their very nature, icons are different from any other kind of picture: they are images of saints venerated "with fear and trembling". In the Catholic Church, paintings of religious subjects are primarily didactic; they are "the Bible of the unlettered" in the words of Gregory the Great. In the Orthodox Church, they are an effective witness to the faith; St John Damascene maintained that they "contain a mystery and, like a sacrament, are vessels of divine energy and grace". Icons are in painting what the Holy Scriptures are in writing: an aesthetic form of the truth, which is beyond the understanding of man and cannot be comprehended by the senses. St John Damascene declared: "Through the intermediary of sensible perception, our minds receive a spiritual impression and are uplifted towards the invisible divine majesty." Icons were revered like the relics of the saints and some were famous for the miracles they performed.

For centuries, icons were painted by priests, who did not sign their work. The 8th Nicene Council stated that "icon painting was not invented by painters; it is, on the contrary, an established institution and tradition of the church." Before setting to work, the painter purified himself by fasting, prayer, confession and communion. Taking a small panel of birch, pine, lime or cypress wood, he smoothed a plane area, leaving a border, which formed a natural frame separating the image from the outside world. Two slats of wood, placed behind, prevented warping. The painter stuck a thin piece of tissue over the planed surface and covered it with a layer of gesso to fix the natural colours, which where often ground with holy water and saints' relics. He varnished the painted image with boiled linseed oil, which heightened the colours for a while, then slowly but surely dulled them. The finished icon was blessed, whether it was placed on the iconostasis* or wall of the church, or whether it was hung in a private house in a special corner with an oil lamp lighted night and day before it.

An icon is a representation of the celestial

* The iconostasis is a wall that separates the congrega-
tion from the place where the priest celebrates the divine
sacrifice. It took its final form in the 14th century,
when it fulfilled the functions of the frescoes that could
not be painted in churches built of wood. It comprised
five superposed registers. The Annunciation and the
Four Evangelists were painted on the leaves of the
central door; large icons hung on either side depicting
the Mother of God, the patron saints of the sanctuary
and the feast to which it was dedicated; on the enta-
blature, the Last Supper. On the second register, Christ
was depicted on a throne between the Virgin and St John:
near the Saviour were ranged the archangels, Michael
and Gabriel, and the apostles, Peter and Paul, followed
by other saints and martyrs. The third register was
reserved for the twelve great liturgical feasts from the
Nativity to the Assumption, the fourth for the prophets,
and the fifth for the patriarchs.

world in terms of the terrestrial, a window opened on eternity. Obviously, it did not attempt an imitation of reality. A majestic, hieratic style removed it from our familiar world and there was no third dimension.

The subjects were taken from the Old and New Testaments, scenes from the life of Christ, the Virgin, patriarchs and saints. In spite of canons that were rarely disregarded, all the icons on a particular subject were not identical, even when they belonged to the same period and the same school. The main outlines remained unchanged, but the variety of treatment is extraordinary; it was a free interpretation, an expression of the artist's personality, his faith and talent, sometimes even his genius.

Decorative motifs were probably the only form of painting that existed in Russia before Vladimir, Prince of Kiev, was converted to Orthodox Christianity in 989 and invited Byzantine artists to his capital to build churches and paint sacred pictures. There is no mistaking the origins of the Russian icon. Very few works of these first masters, whose existence we know of through the chronicles, have survived to this day. Russian artists soon succeeded them and for seven centuries schools with an astonishing variety of forms and colours flourished all over the country. Unfortunately, the icons are not signed or dated and the paintings, like their painters, travelled afield. There is general agreement about some of them, but the specialists, all with equally cogent arguments, are far from ending their discussions on many others. It is all the more difficult to separate and characterise the schools because so few examples have survived from some of them that it is impossible to draw any definite conclusions. A large number of works were destroyed during internal struggles and wars against the Mongols, Swedes and Poles; time and neglect completed these depredations.

Icons from Kiev are rare. When the town was taken by the Mongols in 1240, the holy images that were saved were scattered throughout the country. Their style was still strongly influenced by Byzantine examples; the figures stand facing the observer and their feet do not touch the ground. But they were already beginning to lose some of their unreality and becoming sturdier and more natural, though sometimes rather awkward at the same time. The *Virgin Orans* (pl. 1) shows that the 12th century painter had already broken with strictly Byzantine conventions; the form is traditional but the Virgin has become more human.

The schools of Suzdal and Vladimir lasted from the 12th to the 15th century. The rare icons attributed to them have a certain elegance in spite of the sometimes naïve style of the images, which tried to imitate the hieratic manner of Byzantium. From the 13th to the 17th century at Yaroslav, a general tendency towards ornamentation and detail developed.

A remarkable school developed at Novgorod from the 11th century until the town was annexed to Moscow by Ivan III in 1471 and the population was decimated by Ivan the Terrible in 1570. This independent republic escaped domination by the Mongols, who conquered

Russia and ruled the country for two centuries. Trade brought it foreign ideas as well as prosperity and in the beginning Novgorod made use of Byzantine artists. The style of its painting changed rapidly. The icons were powerful and luminous and their composition simple. Without losing any of their dignity or saintliness, the figures became like thick-set men. The colours were pure and vigorous, with the brilliance of vermilion added to them. The artists were realists so far as the genre allowed them. The *Archangel Michael* (pl. 2), late 13th century, is no longer painted frontally and is looking sideways; the heavenly being has descended onto earth and become a Russian. Although the *Prophet Elias* (pl. 3), late 14th century, is still faithful to a more hieratic convention, it is decidedly humanised. The 14th and 15th centuries were the golden age of painting at Novgorod. The subjects remained precise and the compositions clear. The faces became oval and the heads were adorned with thick hair and the eyes smiled. A marked tendency towards rationalisation is noticeable. Red, yellow and blue were blended in a hitherto unknown harmony. The classic theme of *St George* (pl. 11) was treated at the beginning of the 15th century in iridescent colours and with a simplicity of composition that is extremely forceful. The *Entry into Jerusalem* (pl. 12), late 15th century, marks the end of an accomplished art, which was cut short before it had time to decline.

There were icon painters working in Moscow from the late 12th century. A century and a half later, it asserted its supremacy over all the other parts of the country. After the Turks captured Constantinople in 1453, Moscow became the "third Rome". It was already the political capital; now it was the acknowledged religious capital too. It was at Moscow that the Russian icon reached its heights.

A human naturalism appeared even in the earliest works, which developed in various ways until its finest expression came in the work of Andrei Rublev. Then, like every artistic form, it declined into the affectations of mannerism. As early as the 13th century the figures of the Russian saints, St Boris and St Gleb (pl. 3), took on a Russian appearance; they became men of its soil, and their human and indigenous character is unquestionable.

Three names stand out in the history of the Moscow School. These masters were important for their paintings and the influence they exerted. It should never be forgotten that the painters did not work on their own, but in groups, where the personality of the atelier chief made itself felt in no uncertain manner.

Theophanes the Greek (1340 ?-1410 ?) came from Constantinople. He brought a new strength and intensity to icon painting. His proud, austere dynamism and sombre colours endowed his precise draughtsmanship with an inner power that was new. In his early paintings, there is no mistaking the stern Byzantine origins of his art, but he tempered it later with humanity and even a certain gentleness that was characteristic of the art of his adopted country. Just as El Greco became a Spanish painter,

Theophanes the Greek became a Russian artist. The *Virgin of the Don* (pl. 6) in its simplicity and finish possesses a grace that is reminiscent of some Italian primitives. The composition and harmony of colours in his *Dormition of the Virgin* (pl. 7) are undeniably impressionistic.

Andrei Rublev (1360 ?-1430 ?) was the greatest of the icon painters. This monk had a certain affinity with his contemporary, Fra Angelico. No painter before Rublev had communicated his serene humanity; suffering, trials, fear and terror gave way to hope, gentleness and expectation. In the *Saviour* (pl. 9), Christ who until then had been painted as the "Redeemer with an angry eye", became lovable, friendly and human. This new conception of the image "not made by human hands", since it was derived from a prototype that, according to tradition, God sent to Abgar IV, king of Edessa, was the first to show a Christ pitying the miseries of men. Andrei Rublev's masterpiece is the *Trinity* (pl. 10), which follows the traditional Byzantine iconography of the theme with the three angels, who visited Abraham to tell him that he should have a son, and the patriarch offered them cakes of fine flour, butter, milk and a young calf, specially prepared for them (Genesis XVIII). The theological idea is transposed into a poetic vision. The composition conveys a striking conception of spiritual unity by the slow, steady rhythm of its lines and colours. The rounded form of the heads and the long, oval faces are human and yet they possess a refinement unusual in this lower world. Rublev's *Trinity* is one of the great moments in the history of art. He developed the style of Theophanes the Greek without weakening it; but he introduced into the world of the icon a spiritual richness, a simplicity and a tenderness that were harmonised in an exquisite equilibrium.

This divine humanity is a characteristic of the Moscow School, as in the *Annunciation* (pl. 8), for example, painted in the late 14th century. The end of the 14th and beginning of the 15th century was the great period of Russian icon painters and also, incidentally, the great era of Russian saints.

Denis (1440 ?-1508 ?) developed an even purer art. He was influenced by Russian masters and also Byzantine artists who had fled to Moscow after the fall of Constantinople. His figures were tall and slender, his style elegant and delicate in which pale colours were harmonised with half tones. Refinement was taken to its limits in the *Crucifixion* (pl. 14), where delicacy comes near to insipidity. Decadence was not far off.

In 1547, a huge fire destroyed Moscow. New icons had to be painted to replace the ones that had been burnt and artists were summoned urgently from every part of the country. The Council of the Hundred Chapters in 1551 tried to protect traditional forms; it enjoined strict rules on artists that were laid down in manuals accompanied by descriptions and models. Laymen replaced monks; they signed their works and were concerned with establishing a solid reputation for themselves.

At the end of the 16th and beginning of the

17th century, a family of rich merchants, the Stroganovs, commissioned small sized icons, which created a decorative style rather like the Persian miniature. These charming little paintings, a delight to the eye with their fascinating detail, were the last flash of a dying tradition which was degenerating into exuberance and prettiness. *Virgin of the Catacombs between SS Nicetas and Anastasia* (pl. 15) with its precious meticulousness is characteristic of this school.

In the 17th century, Simon Ushakov (1626-1686) was influenced by the backgrounds, perspective and realism of western Catholic painting. His works are pleasing, but they are pictures of religious subjects rather than icons.

Other centres of artistic activity in Russia should not be passed over in silence. Painting at Pskow from the 14th to the 16th century retained a sombre, archaic colouring; its figures are small and live in a symmetrical world dominated by dark green. From the 14th to the end of the 15th century, a schematic style was typical of Tver, in which forms were painted in pale colours and remained rather crude. The artists of Vologda from the end of the 13th century to the end of the 17th century were awkward, but there is often a touching fervour in the inelegant draughtsmanship of images like the *Virgin and Child* (pl. 4) painted in the late 13th century. Further away, the Northern School, with its simple, naïve drawings in clear, unblended colours, flourished from the beginning of the 14th century. There is nothing emotive about the technique of the *Entombment* (pl. 13), late 15th century, but the preciseness with which the tragic scene is depicted is in itself profoundly moving.

When Johannes Piscator's Bible arrived from Amsterdam with nearly three hundred engravings, the tsars turned against the old conventions and gave orders, with arguments to which there was no reply, that Russian artists should imitate the style of western painting. The ancient icons were destroyed or repainted. Only the sect of the Old Believers, who had refused to accept the reforms of the Patriarch Nikon in the middle of the 17th century and who were persecuted as a consequence, remained faithful to the images of the past. For a time, the old Russian painting disappeared, which contains some of the finest chapters in the history of world art, and was not rediscovered until the twentieth century.

LIST OF PLATES

5. THE PROPHET ELIAS. Novgorod School, Late 14th c. *Tretyakov Gallery, Moscow.*

6. VIRGIN OF THE DON. Theophanes the Greek, Moscow, Late 14th c. *Tretyakov Gallery, Moscow.*

7. DORMITION OF THE VIRGIN. Theophanes the Greek, Moscow, Late 14th c. *Tretyakov Gallery, Moscow.*

8. THE ANNUNCIATION. Moscow School, Late 14th c. *Tretyakov Gallery, Moscow.*

9. THE SAVIOUR. Andrei Rublev, Moscow, Early 15th c. *Tretyakov Gallery, Moscow.*

10. THE TRINITY. Andrei Rublev, Moscow, Early 15th c. *Tretyakov Gallery, Moscow.*

11. ST GEORGE. Novgorod School, Early 15th c. *Tretyakov Gallery, Moscow.*

12. ENTRY INTO JERUSALEM. Novgorod School, Late 15th c. *Tretyakov Gallery, Moscow.*

13. THE ENTOMBMENT. Northern School, Late 15th c. *Tretyakov Gallery, Moscow.*

14. CRUCIFIXION. Denis, Moscow, Late 14th c. *Tretyakov Gallery, Moscow.*

15. THE VIRGIN OF THE CATACOMBS BETWEEN SS NICETAS AND ANASTASIA. Stroganov School, Moscow, Early 17th c. *Tretyakov Gallery, Moscow.*

3

4

5

6

7

8

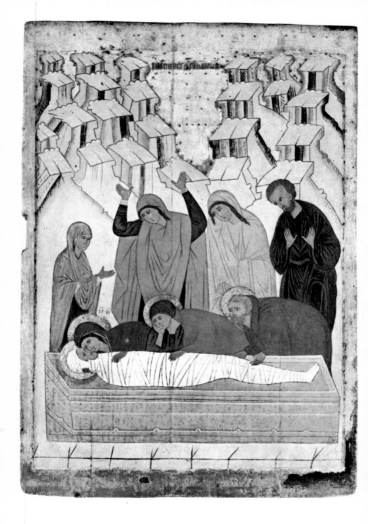

13

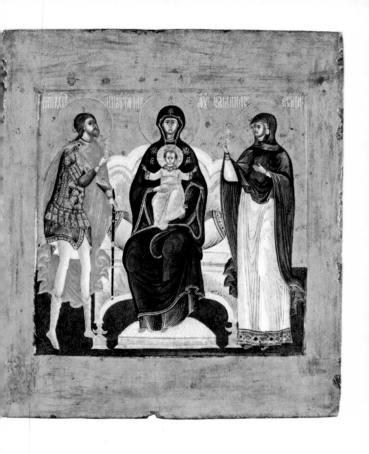